Civic Responsibilities

Karen Kenney

rourkeeducationalmedia.com

*Scan for Related Titles
and Teacher Resources*

Before Reading:

Building Academic Vocabulary and Background Knowledge

Before reading a book, it is important to tap into what your child or students already know about the topic. This will help them develop their vocabulary, increase their reading comprehension, and make connections across the curriculum.

1. *Look at the cover of the book. What will this book be about?*
2. *What do you already know about the topic?*
3. *Let's study the Table of Contents. What will you learn about in the book's chapters?*
4. *What would you like to learn about this topic? Do you think you might learn about it from this book? Why or why not?*
5. *Use a reading journal to write about your knowledge of this topic. Record what you already know about the topic and what you hope to learn about the topic.*
6. *Read the book.*
7. *In your reading journal, record what you learned about the topic and your response to the book.*
8. *After reading the book complete the activities below.*

Content Area Vocabulary
Read the list. What do these words mean?

citizen
civic
community
democracy
draft
election
ensure
represent
volunteers

After Reading:

Comprehension and Extension Activity

After reading the book, work on the following questions with your child or students in order to check their level of reading comprehension and content mastery.

1. *How does voting represent power for a citizen? (Infer)*
2. *What are some ways citizens serve their country? (Summarize)*
3. *Why is it important to respect others even if they share different beliefs and values from yourself? (Asking questions)*
4. *Are taxes necessary? Why or why not? (Summarize)*
5. *What are some ways you could volunteer in your community? (Text to self connection)*

Extension Activity

Part of being a responsible citizen is helping others in your community. Think of the ways you could help those in your community. Could you host a food drive? A coat donation? Donate to an animal shelter? Create a plan and write a letter to your principal asking permission to host your event. Make sure you explain when, why, how, and where your event will take place.

Table of Contents

What Is a Civic Responsibility?

You have been chosen to serve on a jury. While in court, you and other jurors listen to the case. When it is time to decide, the jurors discuss the case in private. Finally, the group comes to a decision and announces it to the judge. They found the person on trial not guilty.

A trial by jury is part of the democratic process. Serving on a jury is a **civic** responsibility. It is an important duty for all U.S. citizens.

During a court case, jury members follow instructions from the judge.

Being a **citizen** is an honor that connects all Americans. They belong to a country that values freedom, liberty, and equality. But it takes work to make a **democracy** happen. Civic responsibilities are the ways you can help your country and fellow citizens.

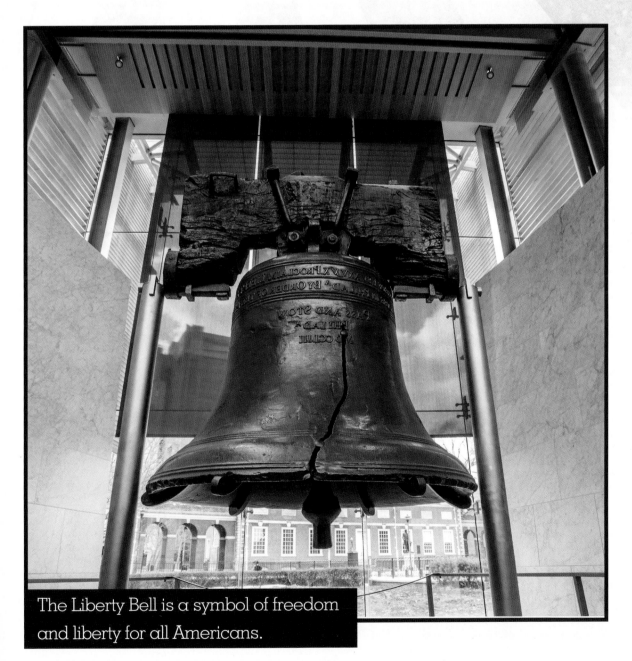

The Liberty Bell is a symbol of freedom and liberty for all Americans.

The U.S. Constitution guarantees our rights as citizens. It defines the basic rights of people in the United States. These rights include the freedoms of speech, press, and religion. People have the right to a trial by jury. They also have the right to vote. Other rights **ensure** different freedoms to people in the United States.

The U.S. Constitution gives citizens the right to freely speak their opinions in public.

These rights come with responsibilities. One is to protect and defend the U.S. Constitution. The United States needs the support of its citizens to make a democracy work.

The U.S. Constitution is the basis of the U.S. government.

Being Involved

A democratic country is ruled by the people. Every person is considered equal. Each voice decides how the country functions. Citizens participate in their government by voting.

Voting is a right given to people who are at least 18 years old. During an **election**, different leaders say they want to serve in the government. These leaders have different ideas of what is best for their **community**, state, or their country. Citizens can choose leaders with values and interests similar to their own. The elected leaders **represent** the needs of the people.

At first, only white men could vote in the United States. In 1869, African American men gained the right to vote. In 1920, women gained the right to vote as well.

The Fifteenth Amendment gave many legal rights to African Americans.

Citizens must understand the issues that affect their communities. Is there a problem with gangs? Should it be easier to recycle plastic? Are there enough jobs in the area? Knowing what needs to be fixed is important. It helps voters make good decisions. The right person in government can help solve these problems.

A community in need of jobs will choose a leader who they believe can help solve the problem.

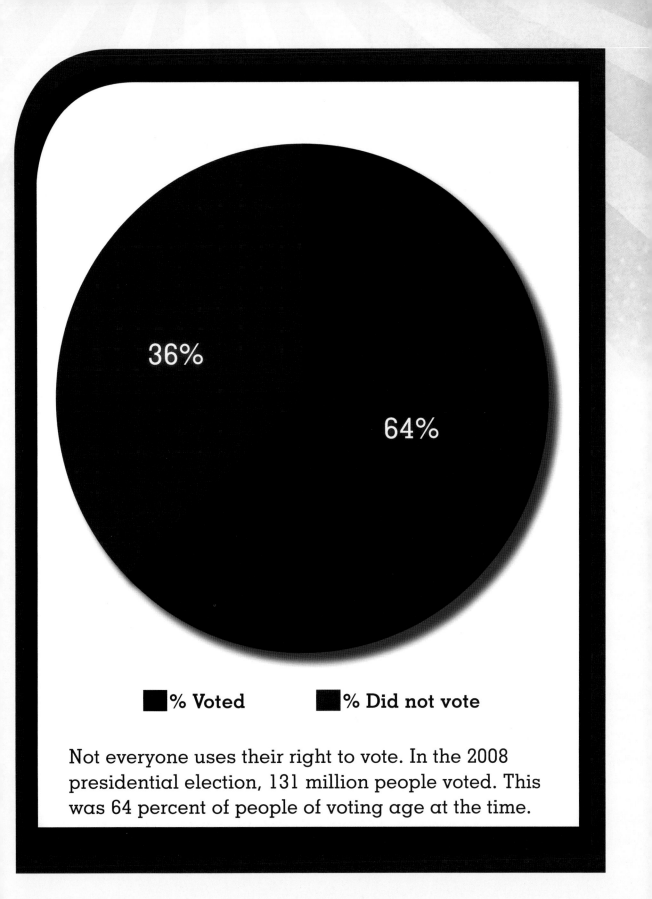

36%

64%

■% Voted   ■% Did not vote

Not everyone uses their right to vote. In the 2008 presidential election, 131 million people voted. This was 64 percent of people of voting age at the time.

Respecting and Helping Others

A good citizen respects other citizens. People with different cultures, religions, and opinions live in the United States. If you do not like a leader in power, it is your right to voice that opinion. But it is also your responsibility to respect others' opinions.

One way to respect others is to obey the law. Laws are there to protect the community. Following laws keeps you and others safe.

Driving over the speed limit puts others in danger. Good citizens follow the rules, to keep their communities safe.

13

The U.S. Postal Service operates in communities all across the United States.

All citizens must also pay taxes. Taxes come out of your pay from a job. You also pay taxes when you buy a new toy at the store. Taxes pay for the government and the things it brings to your community. Taxes pay for roads, schools, parks, and mail service. They also pay for police, fire departments, and the U.S. Army.

Volunteers pack up clothes and other goods for people in need.

Some people in your community need extra help. They may not have enough food or be able to afford a warm coat. It is a civic duty to help others. **Volunteers** can help by serving food at a shelter or shoveling a sidewalk for an elderly person. The whole community benefits from the help of volunteers.

Sometimes the government requires a citizen to be involved in a jury. Every citizen is guaranteed the right to a trial by jury. This means that other citizens will listen to a person's case. The jury decides if that person is guilty or not guilty. It is one way to keep trials fair. A judge cannot have too much power if a jury is involved.

A judge cannot tell the jury his or her opinion during a trial.

Jurors are chosen at random by the government. But not all people selected will actually serve on a jury.

In times of war, soldiers are needed to serve in the military. The government can **draft** men to serve if necessary. If drafted, men must report to the military to defend the United States. It is their responsibility to assist their country.

The last draft was for the Vietnam War.

U.S. Military Drafts

Dates	War	Men Drafted
September 1917 – November 1918	World War I	2,810,296
November 1940 – October 1946	World War II	10,110,104
June 1950 – June 1953	Korean War	1,529,539
August 1964 – February 1973	Vietnam War	1,857,304

Citizens enjoy many rights in the United States. They can freely speak their opinions and practice different religions. Many people want to live in the United States. All U.S. citizens have civic responsibilities. It takes many people to make a democracy work.

Glossary

citizen (SIT-i-zuhn): a person who has the right to live in a certain country

civic (SIV-ik): government and citizenship

community (kuh-MYOO-nuh-tee): a group of people living in the same place

democracy (di-MOK-ruh-see): a type of government in which a country's people choose their leaders

draft (DRAFT): when a person is made to join the military during a war

election (i-LEK-shuhn): the process of making choices through votes

ensure (en-SHOOR): to make sure something happens

represent (rep-ri-ZENT): to speak or act for someone else

volunteers (vol-uhn-TIHRS): people offering to work without pay

Index

Show What You Know

1. What are some ways you can volunteer in your community?
2. Who can vote in elections?
3. Why is it important to know the issues in your community?
4. What do taxes pay for?
5. Who must register for the draft?

Websites to Visit

www.judiciary.state.nj.us/kids/jury.htm

bensguide.gpo.gov/3-5/election/index.html

kidshealth.org/kid/feeling/thought/volunteering.html

About the Author

Karen Latchana Kenney is the author of more than 80 books for children. She's written about many forms of government and U.S. symbols, like the White House and the bald eagle. Kenney lives in Minneapolis, Minnesota.

Meet The Author!
www.meetREMauthors.com

PHOTO CREDITS: Cover © wavebreakmedia, a katz, spirit of america; Title Page © wavebreakmedia; page 4 © Ireneusc Skorupa - ericsphotography; page 5 © Wasin Pummarin; page 6 © ericcrama; page 7 © Koele; page 8 © Daniel Softer; page 9 © Library of Congress; page 10 © KLH49; page 11 © Jen Thomas; page 12 © Oliver Le Queinec; page 14 © Captainflash; page 15 © Steve Debenport; page 16 © junial; page 17 © ktmoffitt; page 18 © Ammit; page 19 © U.S. Marine Corps/ Wikipedia; page 20 © Chris Parypa Photography

Edited by: Jill Sherman

Cover by: Nicola Stratford, nicolastratford.com
Interior design by: Jen Thomas

Library of Congress PCN Data

Civic Responsibilities/ Karen Kenney
 (U.S. Government and Civics)
 ISBN 978-1-62717-685-9 (hard cover)
 ISBN 978-1-62717-807-5 (soft cover)
 ISBN 978-1-62717-923-2 (e-Book)
Library of Congress Control Number: 2014935461

Printed in the United States of America, North Mankato, Minnesota

Also Available as: